Tapestry of Verses

Babara S. Khan

BookLeaf
Publishing

India | USA | UK

Presentation by *BookLeaf Publishing*

Web: www.bookleafpub.com

E-mail: info@bookleafpub.com

ISBN: 9789358314144

First edition 2024

ACKNOWLEDGEMENT

Writing a poetry book is a journey of heart and soul, and it's a privilege to express gratitude to those who have supported and inspired me along the way.

I would like to express my deepest appreciation to:

My family, for their unwavering love and encouragement, which is the foundation of my creativity.

My friends, who have been a constant source of inspiration, motivation, and understanding.

The countless poets and writers who have come before me, and whose works have shaped my perspective and style.

Ashes

A whole populace
Of souls
seeking momentary respite
For permanent pains…
Finding fixes
To fill their voids;
Building homes
In people and thoughts and places…
Feeding lies

To themselves
And to others…

And then ,

They light the match
That once burnt them down
And savour the ashes
Crumbling to the ground.

Fragments

There's a fragment of you
In every person
You have met and loved
Laughed with and cried for …
And when you look
Deep into your heart,
You'll find a mosaic;
Of similar fragments
Of all such pieces put together …

Some could be vivid and bright,
While others yellowed and covered
With the light dust of eons that have passed by;
While some are still weaving their way through
To fit and blend into tiny spaces and voids…

And what binds them
And keeps them from falling apart
Is the time spent,
The memories shared
And how each one has shaped you
To be who you are today.

Silence & Shards

When you take a look inside
Sitting in silence not quite comforting
You often realise…

That the parts of you
That you thought were healed
That you thought were there no more
Were just hidden beneath a band-aid
And packed away in hopes
that the broken pieces would simply fade
away…

But now you see them
Lying scarred on the floor of your bleeding heart
Scratching deeper at the cuts that already exist
Tearing into you every time your heart beats…

And you sit there
Staring at the fragments and the shards
Telling them to mend and heal
but they just lie there
Scratching your heart
Every time it beats

Knots

There are some knots
That simply get tighter
The more you try
To loosen them up
The stronger they hold…

And then you're left
With bruised fingers
Numb hands
Blank minds
And tarnished souls…

Let them be
They'll sway a bit
Rest a little more
And when the time is right
Loosen up
And finally breathe and unfold.

Serendipity

You crept up
Suddenly
Sporadically...

Like a flower on a warm spring day
After waiting for the snow to melt...
Like the sun's rays
You beamed a light
In my heart, I did not think I could love
After feeling so torn apart...

You said my name and replaced
Every bad memory,
The past melted
And rolled off my shoulders…

Has this feeling been hiding beneath me
All this time?
I don't think I can hide this smile
Of mine
What is this feeling you've caused?

I can not place it
But if I had to try
I'd call it *hope*…
How funny to think
Someone who was not here before
Could become the reason

My heart is warmed
My smile is bright
And my laugh is loud…

Since you seeped in
Innately
Definitely…

Eternal *or* Ephemeral

Some things
seem eternal
But are ephemeral
As whispers in the wind…
Creeping up sporadically
Like a flower
On a warm spring day…
A tapestry of time
Threads of love entwined
Petals of a bouquet
Fall off and decay…

Laughter and tears
Memories of old times
Bonds and tales
Some that fade off
Others that forever stay…

Each whisper, laughter and touch
Tender moments shared
Always mean so much
Whether they stay or eventually fleet
Hold on to them
For these are memories
That make you complete.

My Dose of Dopamine…

And yet
Time and again
My thoughts find a way
To enclose you in its embrace…

Dear friend,
The bestest one of them
Do we smile and say 'hello',
Or
Do we exchange glances
Lingering on nostalgia between strangers?

Come, plop on the couch
And let us relive that comfort once more…

For it's you I always miss
It's you my heart forever seeks;
I sit beside you
The dopamine hits me instantly
The laughter rings so true
And I unfold all my stories untold…

While I wait in silence
For these moments to pass
And for you to leave
Once again.

Faith. Hope. Life. Love.

F a i t h
A sense of peace and calm
Which doesn't let you go
and tells you to simply hold on…

H o p e
A glimmer, a light, a spark
It's the path to a new morrow,
a fresh day, a different start…

L i f e
A journey, a voyage, a ride
It takes you through highs and lows
Teaching you to take all in your stride…

L o v e
Passion, pure and strong
It's faith & hope
which adds meaning to your life
The purpose you keep moving on…

Waves & Memories

Just like the waves
Lash at the shore
Your memories rush in
Smouldering my heart…

They soothe a little
They burn a bit
There's silence that lingers
There's chaos that remains…

And while the waves settle…

My heart skips a beat;
A murmur, a giggle, a caress
Whispers in the wind,
Symphony of emotions; my soul cascades.

When You Love Someone...

If you ever love someone
There's just one way
To show them you really care
Make them more
Of what they already are…

More happy
Than they've ever been...
More confident
To pursue their dreams ...

More calm
To hear their heartbeats...
More peaceful
To see the beauty in things…

More vocal
To express their feelings...
More open
To receive life's blessings...

More aware
Of their own faults and flaws
More brave
To walk the untrodden path.

Seasons of the Heart...

Just like flowers
The heart has its seasons…

It blooms,
bright and colourful,
It blossoms,
promising and blissful,
It chokes,
dark and forlorn,
It yields,
anew and wishful,

It withers,
dull and torn,
It wilts,
old and bygone…

So tell me…
Can you see it enraptured
And
Can you see it fold?

Will you love my winter
As you loved my gold?!

When Souls Connect

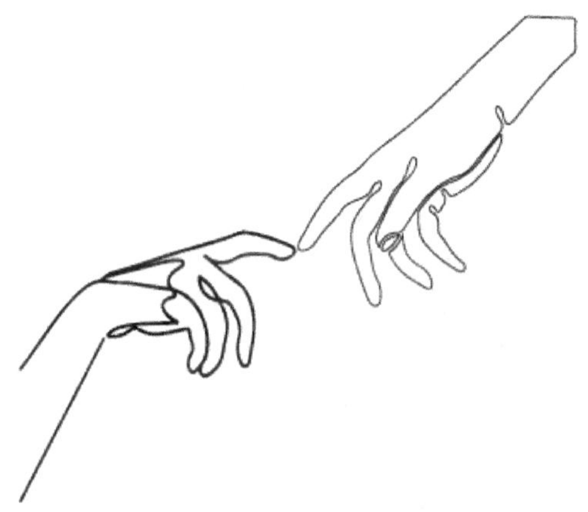

And then are times
When suddenly
Your soul connects
With people you have just known…

They see you, understand you
And unlike anyone else
Can look
Deep into your soul

There's a comfort
When you're together
A bond
Beyond words ever bespoke…

They bring peace,
confidence and happiness;
pouring light
Into corners dark as coal…

They hold out a hand
And at times a mirror
Showing you what you might've ignored
And helping you feel whole…

And then there's a change
Both subtle and deep
Coz you see things differently
and you slowly start to mould…

Hold on to them
For they come once in a lifetime
They're the best kind of people you meet
Coz not everyone can connect to your soul…

My World of Blue

In a sky full of rainbows
You are my world of blue…

Dark,
with a hint of Prussian,
You're the storm
I want to embrace…

Azure,
Filling my senses
Somewhat calm
Somewhat outraged…

Cyan and Sapphire,
Beautiful, bright and benevolent
With precious moments
Like a floral bouquet…

You're the Sky and the Arctic
Inspiring and infinite
A mystery I love to unravel
A pathway to my escape!

When Storms Subside

And in the end
When all your storms subside…

There's a part of you
That's been born,
There's a part
That quietly died…

There's power
You never knew existed,
There's valour
Which pulled you through…

There's voices
That scream and wail and shout
There's silence
So deep and true…

There's a 'You'
That seems to be missing
There's a 'You'
That's newly born…

So
When your storms subside,
Look around,
Look within,

For perhaps the storm
Has taken away a lot
It has definitely
Something to life!

If Dreams Could Scream...

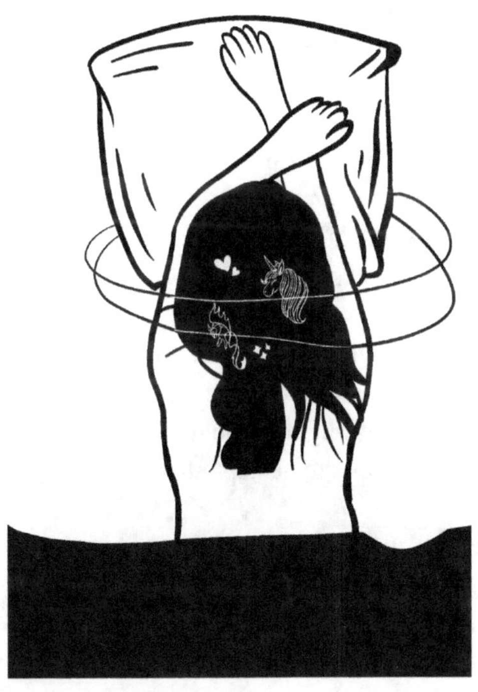

If dreams could scream
If memories could bleed
What would they call you?
What reflection would you see?

Would it be a murderer?
With blood on your hands,
Slaughtered hopes and desires;
Of whimsical, utopian strands

Would you hear a wail
A whisper, a cry?
Perhaps some laughter
A little manic; shrill and high.

A little something, have you killed,
For something else to survive?
A little something that had to die?
For another one to be kept alive.

Each one is a monster
A chimera deep within
So choose to be a warrior
To fight your own demon.

You...

The capacity to love
Is always within you...
The people you love
don't define that capacity
They are but a medium;
A place, a person, a face
to express that emotion that flows within you..

But how you love,
how much you love,
is you... all you... only you.

Poetry Inside Your Soul

You asked me
To look for poetry
Inside your soul
And so I did…

I found words
Hidden in your silence ...
Laughter
Ringing through your smile...

Secrets
Shaded by your lashes ...
Passion
In the darkness of your eyes...
I dug a little deeper
Into your scars and wounds
And found some open and scarred
Bleeding red and bleeding blue...

Your sighs and your murmurs
Sang a tale of their own...
Your chuckles and your chortles
Are the younger you, completely unknown…

I stay a little longer
Looking here and there
For it's not poetry that I seek
It's you, so raw and completely bare.

Loving Darkness...

I always feared darkness
Until you taught me
There's more to it
Than terror and fright...

That beauty isn't
only at morn
That peace doesn't
Always need light...

You opened the windows
And made me
Look at the darkness in the eye
And feel its power and its might...

And amongst the shadows that lurked
I found a serene and silent pace
Where dreams gently whispered
And worries lost their pace…

 I marvelled at the beauty all around
Feeling both safe and calm
But mostly ,
For the first time
I saw the stars being born!

Heart & Mind...

There are two places
Where you store the people you meet
It's either the heart
Or the mind
To relish, cherish or sometimes let free...

The heart lets you love
With passion
Abandon
Wanton
And no conditions...

But the mind
Oh! The mind is shrewd
For it keeps but pretends to forget
It remembers parts you've once loved about
someone
And parts you perhaps now hate

It keeps your memories
While helping you forget
When and with whom they were created...

The heart is filled with people
Of different shapes, times and places

While the mind
Has those selected few
You might still remember but pretend to forget
Thwarted with your ego and perhaps your pain

So where is it that you keep your people?
Who are the ones you love,
And who are those you pretend to forget?

Burning Bridges…

Tell me
How do people burn bridges
That once connected them
To someone else?

> Are people buildings
> Towers and apartments
> You visit for a while
> And then forget the way
> To reach there?

What does it take
I wonder,
To burn a bridge
Is it a single spark
Of a matchstick
To burn the way
And turn the memories to ash?
Or does it take several attempts
One match for every memory, perhaps?

Tell me
How do people burn bridges
For I've often heard
It's a better thing to do
And yet I wonder
How is it better
When all you do
Is burn and turn to ash?

Recipe for Life

What you need is love
A feeling of warmth
A sense of belonging
Knowing you're not alone ...

And then there is hope
To help you in the darkest times
To pull you up when you feel low
To believe you can and you will…

Add in a bit of faith
Of what comes your way
What stays with you and what goes away
Like grains of sand in a fist too tight...

You'll feel the light deep inside
Taking your hand and guiding you
Showing you that darkness isn't forever
Building hope with every stride…

The doubts seem to fade away
Your foggy mind seems a bit clear
 To the beats and rhythm of life,
You slowly begin to sway...

www.ingramcontent.com/pod-product-compliance
Lightning Source LLC
LaVergne TN
LVHW021313200726
843509LV00012B/1893